BUILDING WITHOUT
A BLUEPRINT

Kanika T. Weeks

Disclaimer

All erudition contained in this book is given for informational and educational purposes only. The author is not in any way accountable for any results or outcomes that emanate from using this material. Constructive attempts have been made to provide information that is both accurate and effective, but the author is not bound for the accuracy or use/misuse of this information.

Table of Contents

INTRODUCTION

If you have the desire to start a business, but you're held back by a lack of entrepreneurial experience or capital, this book is written for you. Also, if you never thought about becoming an entrepreneur, this book will motivate you to consider it. If you have started a small business already, you will find useful tools in this book to make your business better.

Building a successful business doesn't always positively correlate with having business experience. Going down the line of history, you'd find that the principal partners of many famous companies today were inexperienced entrepreneurs when they started. Ralph Lauren, Robert F. Smith, Oprah Winfrey, J.K. Rowling, Wendy Kopp, Howard Schultz among others, were not veteran entrepreneurs when they started their businesses. While I humbly acknowledge that I may not be placed among those mentioned earlier, I also stand as a testament to the power of vision and dedication, not stemming from a family legacy in business ownership. Instead, being driven by passion to make a positive impact.

The success of any business depends mainly on three factors, which are knowledge, skills, and experience. As it is now, you have knowledge and skills; in other words, you have two out of the three major requirements to make a business succeed. There is nothing that can stop you now. You have what it takes to start that business and build it excellently.

When you read through this book, you will learn the basics of starting a business, like forming ideas, determining the target audience, and defining the business. You will also receive information about building viable teams that will run the business with you. Furthermore, you will be exposed to the pitfalls that you need to avoid when starting a business.

This book, written with practical examples and illustrations where necessary, is the right tool you need to begin your business. Regardless of your family background and financial circumstances, you will discover invaluable insights in this book that will lead you in constructing your business, even if you lack entrepreneurial experience and initial capital. As you read through this book, get a journal and a pen to write your thoughts about each of the subjects. So that by the time you're done reading, you'd have gotten enough knowledge to start your business and build it successfully. Let's dive right in.

CHAPTER ONE

THE BUSINESS, IS IN THE DETAILS

This is the first step to achieve when you want to start a business – the business details. What problem do you want to solve in exchange for money? What value do you aspire to deliver to people? Where do you want to locate the business? When do you want the business to commence? What values will guide you in running the business? This chapter will explore these and other fundamental business details.

Product/Service

Business is fundamentally centered around delivering value to people, whether in exchange for monetary transactions by providing valuable services at no charge to the customer. In other words, your business is the solution to someone's problem. Therefore, your product or service is the most crucial thing in your business. It is the reason the clients will part with their money. If the product or service you're offering isn't valuable to people, they won't patronize you, and your business could face challenges in sustaining itself.

Some people believe that to define a product or service that will be valuable to people, you need to do a lot of thinking and brainstorming; however, it can be as easy as observing the people in your environment to discover what they consider to be challenging to achieve but relate to their daily lives and offer to do it for them. For example, Larry Page and Sergey Brin discovered that people couldn't access information as and when due, and so, they built Google. In other words, the whole idea behind Google is to help people find the information they need. That's how simple it can be to define a product or service.

Furthermore, you can define a product or service for your new business by improving an existing solution. You can do this by making the solution more user-friendly or affordable. Also, you can choose to help other businesses make their products better.

When starting a business, it's crucial to select a problem for which you already possess the skills to provide a solution. Individuals with substantial resources may leverage their connections to address identified problems. However, for someone aspiring to start a business, it is essential to possess the necessary skills to independently solve the problem at hand. In other words, *ab initio*, select a problem that you can address yourself.

To determine the problems that you can solve, answer the following questions:

- What is that thing that I do passionately even when no one will pay me for doing it?
- What knowledge have I acquired over time that makes me different from others?
- What can I build with that knowledge that people will find valuable?
- What skills have I developed over time?
- What do my friends say I am excellent at?
- What do I do at my leisure?

The answer to the questions above will reveal products/services that you can offer to people. You must be aware that no idea is stupid. Don't throw away any idea. Unlock the power of your creativity by keeping an idea notebook handy; jot down thoughts as they flow, for within these pages may lie the seeds of your future success. After gathering all the ideas or products that you have defined by answering those questions, you need to analyze them objectively and decide which of them you want to pursue at the moment. It is profitable to pick only one of the possible products, for now, you can choose more products later when your business has found its footing.

Target Market

After determining the product or service that you want to offer people, you need to identify the market where your products or services will be impactful. Market, in this case, doesn't have to be a physical location; it could be virtual. You must realize that having a fantastic product or service is not enough to build a successful business; having the right market is crucial.

You need to find out if there's an existing market for your product or service. Are there people in your immediate environment or virtual environment that offer this same product or service that you intend to offer? How will you differentiate yourself from them?

Knowing the details of the market can help you determine how to package your product or service in a way that will be appealing to potential clients.

Furthermore, you need to know if there's enough demand for the product or service that you choose. To what extent is there a demand for your offering in your local community? If you find limited interest, don't be disheartened—consider the vast online landscape, where the global community might be seeking precisely what you have to offer.

One major feature of any market is competition. Whether online or offline, there will be other people offering a similar product as you are doing. You must also know their strengths and weaknesses and determine how you will make your business unique. You can make your business different from others by enhancing product quality, price reduction, appealing and different packaging, changing your location, making your customer service more excellent, among others. As an illustration, Target and Walmart, although providing similar services, employ distinct strategies. Walmart adopts a cost-focused approach, emphasizing reduced prices, while Target distinguishes itself through an appealing and curated shopping environment. You have to examine the market and then determine how best your business will stand out.

It is crucial that you know the characteristics of the product or service you wish to offer, because this will determine the market for it. Consider, for instance, if your product is tailored specifically for men's footwear. While a potential weakness might be its limited appeal to females, particularly those who are single, there's an opportunity to broaden your market. Instead of excluding single females, explore ways to diversify your product line, introducing styles that appeal to a broader audience. By reimagining potential weaknesses as opportunities for inclusivity, you can expand your market reach and better meet the diverse needs of your customers. The idea here is that the characteristics of your product will determine the right market to push it to.

Mission Statement

After determining the product or service you want to offer and the target market, you need to define and document your business. In other words, you need to begin to structure the business in a way that potential clients and team members will know exactly what the business is about without you having to explain every time. To achieve this, you need to make your mission statement clear, concise and available to your team members and customers.

A mission statement summarizes the essence of an organization. It tells people why the business exists, the primary customers, products or services, the location of the business, growth potential, among others. To write a mission statement, follow the simple steps discussed below.

- **Describe the product or service:** This is the first section of the mission statement, and here you are required to write what your business does. No need to be catchy; just write what your business does. For example, the purpose of my company is to design buildings. Alternatively, my business purpose is to sell shoes. Also, your business purpose can be to provide homes for homeless youth.

- **Describe how your business will achieve the purpose:** This step is a little tricky because what is required here is not the physical operations of your business; instead, you are to give a general description of your business operation. To write this section well, you need to identify one or two of the most important core values of the business, and include them. Some examples that you may consider include: 'ensure comfortability and functionality,' provide a high-quality product,' among others.

- **Write why your business wants to achieve its purpose:** This part of the mission statement describes the reason for the business. In other words, it makes us know the desire behind your business. Sometimes, to write this section effectively, you need to think about why you wanted a business in the first place, or why you chose the product or service you wish to offer.

Explore the following well-known mission statements for inspiration. Use them as a reference while crafting the mission statement for your own business.

Facebook "Founded in 2004, Facebook's mission is to give people the power to build community and bring the world closer together. People use Facebook to stay connected with friends and family, to discover what's going on in the world, and to share and express what matters to them."

Children International: "To connect people around the world in the fight to end poverty. Working together, we invest in the lives of children and youth, build the healthy environments they need to thrive, and empower them to create lasting change in their own lives and communities."

Tesla "To accelerate the world's transition to sustainable energy."

American Red Cross: "To prevent and alleviate human suffering in the face of emergencies by mobilizing the power of volunteers and the generosity of donors"

Starbucks "To inspire and nurture the human spirit – one person, one cup and one neighborhood at a time."

The mission statement is crucial to your business. Ensure that it authentically communicates the truth about your business and remains uniquely original.

Business Goals

Setting business goals is crucial to building a successful business enterprise. Your business goals reflect what you intend to achieve with your business. Goals are essential because they help you to keep being motivated. Also, goals help you to assess the progress you're making concerning your business.

Your business goals should be specific. For example, if you set a goal to raise capital, there is no concrete platform to assess and motivate yourself. However, if you set a goal to raise $25,000 within six months, you have a basis for self-assessment and motivation. In this case, you can tell when you have realized the goal and when you haven't. Also, you can make calculations and know how much more capital you need to raise.

Realism in goal setting is equally important for maintaining motivation and ensuring progress. Don't set goals that you obviously cannot achieve. If you're a new service organization setting a goal to serve the entire rural population within the first few months might be overly ambitious or setting a goal to completely eradicate a problem within the community, could lead to disappointment. Let's say you're launching a new product, setting a goal to become the market leader in just three months may be unrealistically high-reaching and could result in discouragement. Unrealistic goals can lead to disappointment and a sense of failure, even when you are making significant progress. For your service organization aim to increase the number of individuals accessing essential services by 30% within the next year or for your product launch aim for achieving a milestone of 90% customer satisfaction rate within the year or securing 10% market share. When you set unrealistic goals, they become counter-productive. In other words, instead of the goals to keep motivating you, they demotivate you.

Breaking down your goals into smaller, actionable steps is essential for day-to-day operations. For the goal of increasing service access by 30%, you could create monthly objectives, such as identifying and reaching out to 5 new households or hosting bi-weekly community engagement events. Some people call this short-term goal, while others call it action plans. Whatever you choose to call it doesn't matter, what matters is that for all your goals, you define actionable steps that you will take every day that will culminate in the realization of those goals. It is crucial that business owners understand that setting goals doesn't yield any benefit until it affects your daily schedule.

Location

The location of a business significantly determines its success. Location is not only crucial concerning getting the right customers, but it is also essential in attracting the right talents to constitute the team. The traditional concept of a business location has dramatically evolved, especially in the wake of the COVID-19 pandemic. The realization that brick-and-mortar premises may not always be necessary has liberated many entrepreneurs, to think differently about how and where businesses are conducted. This transformation has not only helped in cutting down on overhead costs but also expanded opportunities to attract top talent from across the globe, no longer limited by geographical boundaries. Therefore, whether digitally, in-person or mobile offerings, location is essential to the prosperity of the business.

Before you decide "the where", the location, to choose for your business, you should identify the nature of your business and the demographics of those you intend to serve. A graphics design company, for instance, wouldn't prioritize proximity to suppliers as it relies less on physical raw materials. Conversely, if you are starting a service organization that intends to provide educational development through tutoring or mentoring to youth located within the community, you need to think about accessibility for students and their families before choosing a location for your business. The critical point to note here is that you must select a location that will give you optimal access to services, facilities, and resources that you need to make your business successful.

Some of the critical considerations for selecting a physical business location are style of operation, competition, proximity to other services and target population, demographics, utilities and additional costs, laws and regulations, safety, among others. For those who want to do their business online, you can situate your business effectively by familiarizing yourself with the nature of each platform and its algorithms are akin to choosing the right neighborhood for your brick-and-mortar location. Just as you would access a physical location, evaluate whether a digital platform aligns with your business ethos and can support its growth.

Embracing the flexibility to operate digitally, in-person or mobile is not just a trend but a sustainable shift in the landscape of business. This shift can reduce overhead costs but also significantly expand your reach, helping you empower more people and make a more considerable impact. This is the future of business that champions innovation, inclusivity, and most importantly, service to others.

As you plan your business strategy, it's important to understand the distinct features of digital, mobile, and in-person business models. Each model has its advantages and disadvantages that can impact your operational decisions. To aid you in choosing the right model for your business needs, refer to the simple table below helps clarify the distinct features of these types of business operations.

Table 1: Key Features of Digital, Mobile, and In-Person Business Models

Business Operations	Digital	Mobile	In-Person
Location	Operates online, no physical location required.	Travels to customer locations.	Fixed physical location where customers visit.
Accessibility	Accessible 24/7 from anywhere with internet access.	Accessibility depends on travel and appointment schedules.	Limited by store hours and geographic location.
Customer Interaction	Primarily virtual through emails, chats, or video calls.	Face-to-face at customer's location.	Face-to-face interaction at business premises.
Infrastructure	Minimal physical infrastructure, relies on digital tools.	Requires transportation and portable equipment	Requires a physical store or office space.
Cost	Lower overhead costs due to lack of physical space.	Costs associated with travel and transport.	Higher costs due to rent, utilities, and maintenance.
Scalability	Easily scalable without geographic limits.	Scalability limited by logistic capabilities and travel time.	Scalability often requires physical expansion.
Examples	E-commerce stores, online consulting, etc.	Home repair services, food trucks, etc.	Retail stores, restaurants, local service centers, etc.

CHAPTER TWO

DON'T DESPISE SMALL BEGINNINGS

Every house starts with the foundation; there is no house built yet from the roof. You have to start from where you are and with what you have at the moment and grow till you achieve the business of your dreams. The challenge we all face is that we are used to interacting with 'big' things that we fail to consider how they started. For example, we use Facebook, which has over 1 billion users, but we may not believe that the idea began from someone trying to allow some university students to communicate with each other. Every great thing you see today started small.

"Start small" is not synonymous with "don't set big goals;" instead, it means, begin from where you are and grow. To build a successful business, you need to have great dreams and aspirations. In other words, you have to think big. See your business reaching more customers, taking over the market, and making you comfortable. However, after thinking big, you have to start small. Without starting small, you cannot achieve your big aspirations.

Benefits of Starting Small

* **Less time and energy are required:** It is common knowledge that it is easier to perform a small task than a big one. Thus, it is generally more manageable to start small and gradually expand, rather than starting big. As the proverb goes, *do not try to boil the ocean*. This is a reminder that taking on too much at once can be overwhelming and ineffective, emphasizing the wisdom of starting small and focusing on manageable tasks. For example, if you desire to lose weight, will you begin exercising 3 hours daily or start with doing exercises for 30 mins daily? The first option seems to be more productive, but the truth is it's likely unsustainable for most people. On the other hand, starting with the 30-minute sessions allows you to gradually increase your endurance and commitment. Overtime, you can build over time to the first option,

developing the stamina and perseverance required to maintain such a rigorous routine sustainably. Also, in business, starting small may require less time, energy, and team members than starting big.

- **Increased confidence:** When you start small, you will be less afraid than you would have been if you start big. For instance, if you start a tutoring business working from home with just five clients, you will be more confident than when you begin a tutoring business in a costly office space while trying to manage 100 clients right away. For the first option, you probably don't need to take out a loan, seek grants or investments, and you can grow at a manageable pace. However, for the second option, would likely require significant initial financing, such as loans, grants, or other capital investments, with much of your attention diverted to managing financial obligations and the accompanying overhead costs.

- **Lowered stakes**: When you start small, the risks are lower than when you start big. In other words, when you start small, you can make mistakes and learn from them without any significant effect on your business. However, when you start big, every mistake counts. Also, starting small allows you to test your product/service. If it works, you can build on it; if it doesn't, you can discard it without feeling any pain. When you start big, on the other hand, the products must work because a lot has gone into it.

Starting small is the first step to building a lasting and prosperous business enterprise. For instance, when Amazon began, it was only an online bookstore. Today, Amazon has grown to become an 'everything' store. It is worthy of note that Jeff Bezos, the founder of Amazon, didn't design it to be a bookstore, he wanted it to be an 'everything' store. However, he knew he would fail if he started as an 'everything' store. As such, he began as an online bookstore. The key is to have a big plan but start the execution of the big plan in a small way. According to Lao Tzu, "the journey of a thousand miles begins with one step."

How To Start Small

- **Create a niche for your business: What distinguishes you from others.** Most established businesses appeal to general needs of customers; thus, they leave out customers with specific needs, mainly because the profit of meeting the needs of customers with particular needs is lower than the profit of meeting the needs of customers with general needs. Therefore, small businesses can take advantage of this and create a niche for themselves by attending to customers with specific needs. You should not diversify too much when you're starting; focus on a product/service for a particular group of customers. Furthermore, identifying and concentrating on your niche helps you to increase your strengths and reduce your weaknesses and also develop proficiency and trustworthiness.

- **Innovate:** Innovation is the way to go when you are starting small. You need to observe the market painstakingly to discover a problem that other businesses ignore. Your business should be the solution to an existing problem. Don't be afraid to fix a problem that seems to be hard even when you're just starting. Only make sure that you concentrate on one problem at a time. You can make a lot of money and impact when you're the first to solve a problem.

- **Plan for growth:** the fact that you're starting small doesn't mean that you shouldn't plan for expansion. If you don't plan for development and growth, you will remain on the same spot. Develop a strategy that helps your business evolve over time. When investing in essential resources like hardware or software, choose options that will be useful when your business grows. If you run a nonprofit organization, consider affiliating with groups like TechSoup or Good360, which offer access to technology and product donations for those in need. Having to buy new software and hardware every time your business grows can be daunting. Therefore, envision a larger future from the start, but begin your journey with small, manageable steps.

- **Involve others:** Starting small is not synonymous with do everything yourself. In other words, if there are aspects of the business that you cannot handle at the moment you are starting, you can partner with other businesses to get them done. For instance, if you're running an e-commerce store that sells custom merchandise, it's not necessary to purchase your own printing equipment right away. Instead, you can collaborate with a print-on-demand services such as Printify, Amazon Merch on Demand, and others that handle the production and shipping. This will allow you to focus on the design and sales will the service takes care of the fulfillment. As your business grows you eventually may want to explore acquiring resources to bring some of those tasks in-house. Similarly, for non-profit organizations providing direct services, partnering with established organizations can enhance your service delivery without the immediate need for extensive resources.

Even with the intention to start small, it's common to begin too ambitiously because excitement can lead you to take on too much too quickly. The wisdom of starting small and embracing humble beginnings is a common theme. For example, a passage from the Bible, Zechariah 4:10, advises, *"Do not despise these small beginnings.... It* encourages us there is no other sustainable way to build rather than to start small. Regardless of your faith or background, it's important to value the early, often unnoticed stages of your endeavors, recognizing that they are the foundation of future success.

CHAPTER THREE

ALIGN KEY PARTNERS AND TEAM PLAYERS

Sometimes, people think starting a business means working alone. As such, many new entrepreneurs create their products/services alone. However, it usually doesn't take long for such entrepreneurs to appreciate the importance of having key partners and a functional team to the development of their businesses.

Building the right team can be as daunting as developing the product/service that the business offers. If you pick the wrong team members, you cannot build a successful business, no matter the novelty of the solution you're offering. So also, if you have the right team but don't have a great solution to people's problems, your business will not grow. The point here is that as much as a great product or service is crucial to the commencement and development of any business, so also is having a great team.

Below are some strategies that can help guide you in selecting the right partners and team members for your business.

How To Select the Right Partners And Team Players

- **Define your business:** we spoke extensively about this in the first chapter. You must know what you want before thinking of seeking out partners or building a team. Your business details should determine the kind of people that will work with you, and not vice versa. Some people use their family members and friends as partners and team members without fully briefing them on the business details; this is a poor practice. You need people who are passionate about what the business produces to make it grow. Therefore, the first step to building the right team and having the right partners is to define your business clearly.

- **Quality over Quantity:** For most businesses, there is no stipulated number of team members and partners that are required. Therefore, don't allow people to join your business in haste. Interview them, find out if they believe in you and your dreams for the business. Only choose people who believe that failure is the steppingstone to success; who are willing to work with little motivation. Also, as a start-up, you may not acquire those with big names or high-level skillsets — that's ok. Choose people who are willing to learn and are teachable. It is not the number of team members and partners that is crucial; instead, it is the virtues and values that they contribute to the business.

- **Communicate assertively:** Assertive communication is crucial when building teams and partners for any business. Assertive communication involves telling every team member and partner what you expect from them in detail (the task, deadline, who to report to, among others) and also listening to them. Sometimes, what destroys a business is that the team members don't know their specific roles; they only do what they think is right. *Ab initio*, you must communicate with each potential team member and partner what their roles will be. Also, subsequently, if there's a need to change the positions, you need to let them know in detail and clearly what they are to do. A significant part of assertive communication is active listening. You must be willing to listen to your team members and partners. When they have complaints, or when they are offering some suggestions that can move the business forward. Active listening involves hearing what the speaker is saying without bias, asking questions to be sure you understand what the person said, and acting on what the person has said.

- **Know the strengths and weaknesses of each player:** When you select team members and partners, you must know what they can do well and what they can't do. This will help you when you're to allocate duties to the team members. People always function better when they are given tasks that correlate positively with their strengths; however, they will struggle, or perform poorly if the task is not inversely proportional to their strength.

- **Provide platforms for personal growth:** As I mentioned earlier, you can't have the big names in your industry yet, because their cost will be too much for you to bear. Most likely, when using volunteers or interns these people may have little experience with your business. Therefore, fostering an avenue for growth is essential. Consider providing a book that relates to the task assigned to them and providing in-house training. Additionally, invest in your team members' development by sponsoring attendance to conferences, seminars, among others, that will help them become more effective. Moreover, ensure the work environment is conducive for them to grow.

- **Encourage good interpersonal relationships between team members:** When there are unresolved quarrels between team members, productivity will be hampered. You have to watch out for potential conflict points and resolve them even before they start. Furthermore, you must learn conflict resolution skills. You should never judge a case before hearing all the sides involved. Never let your team members feel that you are partial. Create time for team building activities, games, and other fun things that will make team members interact. In addition to this, design your office space in a way that team members have to see each other often.

You can find the right team and partners by networking, using local community college resources via their small business center, volunteer work programs such AmeriCorps, job seeker agencies and surveying the community where your business will serve. Also, you can advertise the business on different social media platforms.

CHAPTER FOUR

GROW IN SILENCE

As a new entrepreneur, you must aim for growth; you cannot remain where you have always been. You must develop your products, your service, team members, market skills, among others. However, it is always better to grow in silence. Growing in silence doesn't mean not advertising your product/service; instead, it means having an attitude of not competing with anyone who seems to be ahead of you.

Numerous emerging entrepreneurs distract themselves from pursuing their business goals by engaging in unhealthy rivalry and competition. They feel compelled to announce to everyone what they are doing, to gain respect and fit in; however, this isn't necessary. In today's social media driven society, appearances can be deceiving. If you don't have a beautiful office space yet, don't allow another business's online showcase pressure you into making premature, budget unfriendly decisions. Grow at your pace, and learn as you grow.

You don't have to tell everyone about what you do; you only need to tell the right people. Some people would have built their business except that they discussed their plans with people who discouraged them. You should never discuss your business with anyone who isn't making progress in their business, or who has a record of discouraging you from taking giant strides. You have to be careful here, though. As an emerging entrepreneur, you are most likely adventurous; that is, you are passionate about trying new things. However, if you inform someone who has been in business for a while, they can tell you not to take a particular step; that doesn't mean they are trying to discourage you. You must use wisdom, discern between people who want to discourage you and those who don't want you to take a foolish step. Before you select someone to discuss your business with, check what they are doing. Do they have a business? Do they take risks? What is their general disposition towards your business? Do they consider your success a threat to theirs? Among others. In short, *don't take swimming lessons from drowning people.*

Dealing with toxic people who always want to undermine your success is not easy, especially when they are family members. You can use either of the two approaches discussed below.

- **Ignore them:** More often than not, toxic people are also attention seekers, because of their feeling of insecurity. Their actions can be as little as interrupting you when you are speaking, being too loud, and intolerable, among others. When you don't give them the attention they want, then they intensify their actions. In any case, don't allow them to use emotional blackmail on you; pay less attention to them and spend more time with people who encourage you to achieve your dreams. Toxic people don't have to be aware that you're trying to avoid them; you can do that by ensuring that you are always busy. In other words, there is something you have to do per time. It may be as little as catching up with someone, reading a book, having rest, among others.

- **Confront them:** Sometimes, it is essential to stand up to toxic people — especially those who meddle in your business affairs. You can tell them directly that you don't want them around you. Also, you need to stand on your plans. For example, if someone is asking that you spend above your budget, you can tell the person directly that you have a plan, and you won't go beyond that plan for any reason. Moreover, you don't have to wait till toxic people influence you, stand up for others; that way, they may not even come near you at all.

One of the best ways to ensure that you grow in silence is to surround yourself with positive people who desire that your business will develop. Connect with like-minded people offline and online who will provide you with information about opportunities for growth, which include conferences, scholarships, seminars, among others. Have friends that share ideas with you just like you do with them. Also, it is essential to get a mentor.

CHAPTER FIVE

RESPONDING TO 'NOs'

As an emerging entrepreneur, you must be aware that rejection is part of business. Every famous entrepreneur today experienced rejection at one point or the other. One of the programs built by Mark Zuckerberg was closed down by the University management, before he developed Facebook. Oprah Winfrey was rejected at a station before she took on a local show that made her famous. Everyone experiences rejection; it is the way we handle rejection that makes the difference between the great and the small.

If you don't experience rejection, it probably means you are not doing anything novel. Once you attempt to do something unique, some people will not believe in you, and they will reject the idea. As an entrepreneur, rejection can mar or make you. It can be a turning point for success, and can be the path to downfall.

Below are strategies for managing rejection.

- **Express your emotions:** I guess you didn't expect this to be part of the ways to deal with rejection, but it is. You are human; you have to express your emotions. If you don't, you won't get along well with the next steps. Do something that makes you happy, get a coach, talk to a trusted friend, among others. If need be, cry, scream, but don't hurt yourself. Only let your emotions out.

- **Ask Questions:** It's crucial not to allow emotions to overpower you in the face of rejection. After expressing your feelings, you need to be objective. Find out why your business proposal was rejected. Was your proposal dismissed as a result of the uniqueness of the idea or the lack of excellence in its presentation? Either way, you need not beat yourself, because it will not change what has happened. However, when you know exactly why the proposal was rejected, you can prepare adequately for future opportunities.

- **Learn from your mistakes:** Avoid shifting the blame. Take responsibility for what has happened and learn what you should from the events. Often, we feel good when we blame others for our predicaments. When we do this, we don't learn from those mistakes. A constructive approach to dealing with rejection involves identifying areas of improvement and initiating actions to address them. For example, if your proposal was rejected because you lack the skills to adequately articulate your business's mission, goals, or needs, you can set goals and action plans towards developing yourself in that area. In instances where your proposal was rejected, due to lack of community engagement, team talent or strong partnerships, take proactive steps to address these issues. Start by deepening your understanding of the community you aim to serve; attend local events and stakeholder meetings to gain insights and build relationships. Also seek to establish partnerships with other organizations for the sake of enhancing your products/services ensuring that both parties derive mutual benefits from the collaboration.

- **Let rejection fuel motivation:** You need to make up your mind that no matter what, you will see the business through. Each rejection should strengthen your resolve. As I mentioned, every great entrepreneur today was rejected at one point or the other, and their stories motivate others today. Know that your story will also motivate others someday; therefore, don't give up. Try again, after you have made the necessary improvements.

The above tips are useful when you experience rejection; however, before you experience rejection, you must change your mind-set about 'NOs.' View them as steppingstones to success rather than destroyers. Also, don't hate people who reject your business proposals. Conclusively, you must separate yourself from your business. In other words, don't attach your self-worth to the acceptance or rejection of your business. You are a great person, irrespective of the happenings around your business.

CONCLUSION

In this book, I have shown you how to build a business without a blueprint. It does not matter if you're the first in your family or you've never seen done what you're trying to do. In other words, I have established the fact that you can be a successful entrepreneur without necessarily having someone to look up to. I have also shared what you have to do when you're starting a new business.

The tips shared in this book are practical and can help you a great deal. However, knowing the tips is not the ultimate but acting on them. Now that you know about starting a business without any model to look up to, I encourage you to do something meaningful with that knowledge.

Fear is an enemy that will hinder you from taking meaningful action. Conquer fear and reach out for success. The journey will not be smooth, as I already mentioned, but in the end, it will worth it.

I wish you all the best.